Beautiful
HISTORIC IRELAND

Featuring the photography of Michael Diggin,
Bord Fáilte, the Northern Ireland Tourist Board
and Colour Library Books Ltd

Published in Ireland by Gill & Macmillan Ltd
Goldenbridge
Dublin 8

With associated companies throughout the world
© 1993 Colour Library Books Ltd, Godalming, Surrey
Printed and bound in Singapore by Tien Wah Press
ISBN 0 7171 2073 2

Beautiful
HISTORIC
IRELAND

Gill and Macmillan

Ireland is a nation with a long memory. It is possible to have conversations with people who speak of events that happened centuries ago as if they themselves were there. Few nations on earth can match this sense of history and historic perspective, which is to be found as much in the land as in the people.

The first Irish were nomadic hunters who arrived in the wake of the Ice Age some 11,000 years ago. They were replaced in about 5,500 B.C. by farmers, some dim memory of whom might be the source for the legends of the Fir Bolg, a short, dark people with semi-human giants as their slave workforce.

Whatever the origin of the Fir Bolg, the farmers have left their mark on the Irish landscape. They cleared much of the forest which originally covered the land, and they constructed massive tombs for their dead. The greatest of these is Newgrange, in the Boyne Valley. With a diameter of 338 feet and a height of 30 feet, the burial mound is impressive in bulk, an impression heightened by the glistening white quartz with which it is faced. A single tunnel leads into the mound to a burial chamber at the heart of the structure. At sunrise on the day of the winter solstice the sun shines directly down the passage to bathe the burial chamber in an eerie, orange-red glow. Newgrange is only the most striking and complete of hundreds of chambered tombs that lie scattered across Ireland, the oldest reminders of the land's inhabitants.

Legend speaks of the Tuath de Danaan, the followers of the Goddess Danu, supplanting the Fir Bolg, while archaeology has found traces of a new culture, if not a new people, arriving in about 2,000 B.C. These people raised circles and rows of standing stones, some weighing many tons. These impressive monuments can still be seen scattered across the Irish landscape.

But is was not until the Celts overran Ireland that the historic context merged firmly into both legend and landscape. One of the earliest Irish heroic legends tells of Cu Chulainn and his battles against the warriors of Connacht. Many of the places mentioned in the tale can still be visited on the Cooley Peninsula. On the Hill of Tara stand the earthworks and buried foundations which are all that remain of the palace and stronghold of the Kings of Tara, who claimed to be High Kings of Ireland from the dawn of history to the 12th century.

The Celtic era of cattle raiding, local kings and a warrior aristocracy has left numerous traces across Ireland. Indeed, it can be said that modern Ireland is the direct inheritor of the traditions of these proud, artistic and passionate people. Throughout the island can be found raths, fortresses and ruins associated with the Celtic era. It was a time when more than 150 kings ruled their lands, seeking alliances and wars with equal eagerness. The great fortress of Dun Aengus on Inishmore dates to this time. Its complex defences were designed to frustrate the chariot charge, which was a favourite battle tactic of the early Celts.

When the Christian Church arrived in the 5th century new features became established. Monasteries sprang up and their ruins can still be seen. The most distinctive legacy of the monasteries are the round towers, found in no other country. Standing as much as 100 feet tall, the spindle-thin towers may have served as both bell towers and refuges in time of war.

With the coming of the Normans, castles began to be built and these, together with fortified domestic buildings, are the chief historic legacy of the centuries down to the later 1700s. Early castles, built by powerful magnates, tended to be massive creations spreading over as much as two acres. Trim Castle is perhaps the finest example of this style, which linked Ireland into the mainstream of European architecture. As time passed, the fragmentation of landholding and continued troubles led to a proliferation of fortified houses of a peculiarly Irish style. The fine tower house of Bunratty Castle is typical of the type.

Not until the coming of relative peace in the 18th century did historical events in Ireland provide another profound influence on the landscapes and buildings to be seen today. Large estates centering around grand houses became the norm across much of the island, and the fashionable classical style was adapted to Irish tastes, resulting in magnificent country houses. Large and small, these country homes were the epitome of both Irish society and refined taste, the style continuing until well into the 19th century.

In the towns a similar style predominated, and many of Ireland's cities remain classical jewels of 18th- and 19th-century architecture. Unfortunately, the finest of Ireland's historic cities, Dublin, has recently lost much of its old character with the arrival of modern, high-rise developments which have swept away the past. But even this new international style so bemoaned by many is reflecting yet another twist in Irish history, for the growing integration of Ireland and the Irish economy into the international community is being matched by a decline in national styles as companies seek international glitz for their public face.

The latest developments show that historic Ireland is still developing. Just as the massive tomb of Newgrange swept away the primeval forest, and the castle at Bunratty replaced a less sophisticated fortress of the cattle-raiding days, so modern finance is shaping Ireland in its own image. It is a process that will continue for as long as the Irish inhabit Ireland.

Facing page: Gosford Castle, County Armagh, was built in the early 19th century near the site of the ancient stronghold of the Achesons.
Right: Carrickfergus Castle, County Antrim – one of the most complete Norman castles in Ireland. It was begun around 1205 and has been used continuously ever since.
Below: The site of Dunluce Castle, County Antrim, has been fortified since pre-Christian times, but nothing prior to the 14th century now remains.
Overleaf: Belfast Town Hall, built in 1906.

Right: The ruins of Mellifont Abbey, which lie near Drogheda in County Louth. The Abbey was founded by Cistercians from Clairvaux, who came here in 1142 at the invitation of the Bishop of Armagh, who wanted to take advantage of the access to French learning and manuscripts that the monks would bring.

Facing page: Standing 110 feet tall, the round tower at
Monasterboice, County Louth, is about 900 years old.
Above: Muireadach's Cross, at Monasterboice, dates back to the
10th century and is covered in magnificent reliefs depicting
scenes from the Bible. **Overleaf:** Monasterboice.

These pages and overleaf: Newgrange, County Meath. This
huge burial mound is around 4,500 years old and stands on the
northern slopes of the Boyne Valley. The entrance (left) and
retaining stone wall have been restored in recent years to show the
ancient monument in all its former splendour.

Left: The Hill of Tara was once the home of the High Kings of Ireland. Heroic legends and tales of gods revolve around Tara in profusion. The exact nature of the power wielded by the kings in Tara has been much debated and may have been symbolic as much as real. The grass-covered ruins date from many periods, remaining highly charged with atmosphere and imbued with majesty.

Top left: Slane Castle, which was built at the end of the 18th century. **Above and overleaf:** The ruined 16th-century monastery on the Hill of Slane. **Left:** 18th-century Headfort Demesne, on the Blackwater River.

Dublin, the Viking port city founded on the banks of the River
Liffey. **Top left:** The Custom House was built in 1791, gutted in
1921 and subsequently rebuilt. **Above:** The Four Courts,
completed in 1796. **Left:** The General Post Office, headquarters
of the Irish Volunteers during the 1916 Easter Rising.

Dublin. **Facing page:** Dignified Georgian houses on Merrion Square. **Right:** Christ Church, built by Strongbow in 1172 to be his burial place, and much altered since. **Below:** Saint Patrick's Cathedral, which stood vulnerably outside the city walls when it was built in 1190, is now the mother church of the Church of Ireland.

Dublin. **Left:** The impressive Bank of Ireland, which was begun in 1729 as Parliament House, but converted to its present use after the Union.

Below: The façade of Trinity College, built in 1759, when the original Tudor buildings proved inadequate for the growing college.

Facing page: The old College of Science, now part of Government Buildings.

Clonmacnoise Monastery, County Offaly, was founded in 548 and quickly became the finest seat of learning in Ireland. Its period of greatest fame was during the 9th and 10th centuries, after which it went into decline. It was sacked by English troops in 1552 and abandoned. **Facing page:** The High Cross. **Below:** The Nuns' Church. **Overleaf:** An aerial view of the complex. **Right:** The magnificent mansion of Charleville Demesne at Tullamore, County Offaly.

Right: Founded in the mid-12th century, the Cistercian Abbey of Jerpoint, County Kilkenny, was the brainchild of the local kings of Ossory and benefited greatly from their generosity. It was abandoned in 1540 on the orders of King Henry VIII. **Overleaf:** Part of the five-acre ruins of Kells, County Kilkenny. The monastery was founded in about 480, but was entirely rebuilt, together with a castle, in the 12th century, and it is these buildings which remain.

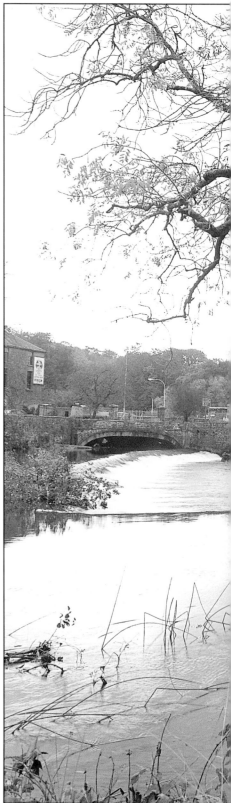

Above: Cahir Castle, County Tipperary, home to the Earls of
Ormonde from 1375 until the line died out in the last century.
Top left, left and overleaf: The Rock of Cashel, ancient fortress
of the Kings of Munster and later a monastic centre of great fame.

Left: Lismore Castle, County Waterford, a largely 18th-century rebuilding of a fortress first erected in 1185, which was for many years the stronghold of the Earls of Cork. **Overleaf:** The round tower of Ardmore, County Waterford, stands 96 feet high, dwarfing the chapel built by Saint Declan in the fifth century.

Above: Blarney Castle, home in the 16th century to Dermot MacCarthy. MacCarthy was the wily chief of Muskerry who kept both sides happy in the wars with soft words. **Right:** Kissing the Blarney Stone, said to confer the power of persuasive speech.

THERE IS NO CHARGE FOR
KISSING THE BLARNEY STONE
REMOVE ALL LOOSE VALUABLES
BEFORE DOING SO

Left: University College, Cork, which echoes much of Cork's Gothic-style architecture, most of which is Victorian in date. **Below:** Bantry House, former home of the Barons of Bantry. **Facing page:** The 18th-century chapel built on the site of the 7th-century refuge of Saint Finbarr on the island at Gougane Barra, County Cork. **Overleaf:** Drombeg Stone Circle, County Cork, thought to date from around 200 B.C.

Above: Beehive monastic cells, over 1,000 years old, on Skellig Michael, County Kerry. **Top right:** An early Christian memorial stone at Reask, on the Dingle Peninsula. **Right:** The Gallarus Oratory, County Kerry, thought to date from the 10th century.

Left: Muckross House, Killarney, a fine 19th-century mansion which has been converted into a folk museum. The gardens are especially charming and well cared for. **Overleaf:** Muckross Abbey, a Franciscan foundation of the 15th century, which was destroyed by Cromwell's troopers.

Left: Carrigogunnel Castle, County Limerick, was once a fastness of the O'Briens of Thomond, but it was blown up in 1691 and has been a ruin ever since. **Below:** Adare Manor, County Limerick, was designed by the second Earl of Dunraven to be the family seat, which it remains. **Facing page:** The Franciscan Friary of Askeaton, County Limerick, which was erected in the 15th century.

Facing page: The towerhouse of Craggaunowen, County Clare, centre of a novel museum which includes reconstructions of ancient buildings, including an Iron-Age farmstead (below). **Right:** Quin Abbey, County Clare, a Franciscan friary founded in 1433.

These pages: The Poulnabrone dolmen on The Burren of County Clare. These remnants of prehistoric burial grounds lie scattered over the region and argue for a sizeable population at the time they were in use.

Facing page: Bunratty Castle, County Clare, was built in 1425 and has now been restored to its original appearance. The nearby cottages (above) have also been restored, recreating a working village of the 19th century.

Right: Kylemore Abbey, on the shores of Kylemore Lough, stands north of the Twelve Bens. The Abbey is the Victorian creation, based on Tudor designs, of Mitchell Henry, a rich northern English merchant. Henry drained extensive areas of lakeside bog for his famous gardens.
Overleaf: The stone fortress of Dun Eoghanachta, on Inishmore, dating from about 500 B.C.

These pages and overleaf: Magnificent Ashford Castle near Cong, County Mayo, the Victorian country home of the wealthy Guinness family. It is centred around a much older towerhouse and now serves as a luxury hotel.

These pages: The ruins of Cong Abbey, County Mayo, which was built in the 12th century by Roderick O'Connor, High King of Ireland, as a refuge for Augustinian canons.
Overleaf: Saint Patrick's Purgatory, County Donegal.
Last page: Croagh Patrick, County Mayo.